SENTINELS
of the
SHORE

By Bill Gately

SENTINELS
of the
SHORE

A Guide to the
Lighthouses and Lightships
of New Jersey

By Bill Gately

Photographs by the author

For information, address:

Down The Shore Publishing Corp., Box 3100, Harvey Cedars, NJ 08008

The words "Down The Shore" and the Down The Shore Publishing logo
is a registered U.S. Trademark.

Printed in China. Second printing with author's revisions.
10 9 8 7 6 5 4 3 2

Cover and book design by Leslee Ganss

Library of Congress Cataloging-in-Publication Data
Gately, Bill, 1954-
      Sentinels of the shore : a guide to the lighthouses and lightships
   of New Jersey / by Bill Gately ; photographs by the author.
            p.   cm.
      Includes bibliographical references.
      ISBN 0-945582-37-4 (hardcover)
      1. Lighthouses -- New Jersey.   2. Lightships -- New Jersey.
   I. Title.
   TK1024.N5G38   1998
   387.1'55'09749--dc21   98-18134
                                                                       CIP

For Linda and Emily

TABLE OF CONTENTS

REFERENCE SECTION

INTRODUCTION

First, a brief definition: A lighthouse is a building, on or near the shore, that exhibits a light high enough above the water to mark hazards, the entrances to harbors, and shipping channels. Each lighthouse is distinguished by a unique signal, indicating the structure's identity and location along the coast.

Before modern navigational equipment, mariners needed this signal information to navigate in the dark of night. Yet lighthouses also aided mariners by day, their painted, characteristic stripes and colors serving as seamarks (also known as "daymarks"). In areas where fog posed a frequent problem, lighthouses were equipped with devices such as horns, whistles, and bells. Offshore, where it was not feasible to build such sentinels, lightships were anchored to mark an approach to land or an obstruction. These vessels displayed a light from either a mast or an onboard tower.

In the days before radio communication and electronics, lighthouses and lightships offered the only hope a mariner had for making a safe voyage.

New Jersey, over the course of its history, contained forty-nine of these sentinels, many of which still stand today. They begin as far north as New York Harbor, continue down along the seacoast and around Cape May, then proceed along Delaware Bay and up the Delaware River. All of them have their own unique histories. Sandy Hook Lighthouse, for example, is the oldest standing and still functioning lighthouse in America, dating back to colonial times. Also, one of the most impressive architectural achievements of its day is located in Highlands: the Twin Lights of Navesink. Because of the ever-changing coastline, several lighthouses originally built close to the water seem to have traveled inland (Absecon Lighthouse, for instance). The reverse is true for other lighthouses that were undermined and eventually swallowed by the sea.

Lighthouse Life

Though the lighthouse itself is simply a navigational aid, it represents much more: It symbolizes man's humanity to man. Many lighthouses are located in idyllic settings — on bluffs high above the sea, for instance, surrounded by trees and overall scenic beauty. It is not difficult to imagine living in such a setting just for the serenity or the view.

Sea Girt Lighthouse

But life at the isolated, wave-swept lighthouses and ocean-stationed lightships presented many hardships and dangers. Keepers remained at their lights through the most terrible winter gales imaginable, and many had to stay for longer-than-normal tours during periods of extended foul weather and especially rough seas. In addition to their routine duties of caring for the wicks and lenses, keepers had to scrape snow and ice from the panes of the lantern room and keep the beam of light visible. And during the worst weather, when wrecks would occur, keepers often had to join in rescue efforts beyond the call of duty. This was particularly true for the crews of lightships, which had to endure much during such storms. Ships would roll so violently that men were thrown from their bunks and panes of glass fell from the mast-mounted lanterns. Also, during icy conditions lightships would become top heavy, creating more danger for a crew that had to chip ice from the superstructure.

For many keepers whose stations were located in areas known for extraordinarily violent waves, their lives depended on whether or not a tower would withstand the constant pounding. Fortunately, some of the nineteenth-century towers had truly impressive engineering. As a guarantee their stones would fit precisely, granite lighthouses were preassembled on land, course by course. The finished stones were then disassembled and shipped to the offshore location for re-assembly. In Minot's Ledge Lighthouse off Massachusetts, for example, each stone was dovetailed horizontally to fit the next. Two-inch steel dowels or pegs were then inserted vertically for attachment to the next higher course. Some of the individual stones weighed as much as two tons. It took years to finish the tower, which is estimated to be as strong as solid rock. But there is an irony here: With all of the engineering, hard work, and expense that went into the construction of Minot's Ledge Lighthouse, little was afforded the soul who so faithfully tended this station. The light had no central heating system or plumbing, and each level of living quarters was another round room providing visual monotony. Also, the first 40 feet of the 100-foot tower consisted of solid wall: Keepers climbed a ladder to the entry door. Minot's Ledge may have been an excellent light for the mariner, but it was a miserable station for the keeper.

The Tower

The design and shape of lighthouses serve to provide both a suitable height for the light and a dwelling for the lightkeeper. In New Jersey's low-lying coastal areas where mariners needed a tall seacoast light, huge cylindrical towers such as Absecon, Barnegat, and Cape May lighthouses were built. In excess of 160 feet tall, these towers are tapered and have thick walls at the base to support their immense weight. (In California, some lightstations on the high cliffs near the sea present the reverse problem: These towers had to be as small as possible to avoid ascending into heavy fog.)

There are many types of lighthouses found in New Jersey. Some display the architecture of their era: Sandy Hook Light has an octagonal, conical design, similar to New London Harbor Light in Connecticut and Eaton's Neck Light in New York, all of which were built in the late 1700s. Lights such as East Point and Chapel Hill Rear have towers atop the dwellings, typical of stations built around the 1850s. Hereford Inlet Lighthouse, built in 1874, is Victorian with stickwork and gingerbread.

The Texas oil rig-style towers, such as Ambrose off Sandy Hook, combine high technology with characteristics of various ous lighthouse designs. The open frame allows ocean waves to pass through the support legs, while the light is displayed 136 feet above the water for maximum visibility. The tower holding the light rises from one corner of the upper platform to allow room for a helicopter landing pad.

New Jersey also has among its lights several "ranges," which were used to mark shipping channels in Sandy Hook Bay and up the winding Delaware River. Ranges consisted of at least two lighthouses: a front light (or "beacon") close to shore and a

Finn's Point Range

rear light (or "range") usually a mile or more behind it. Often an open-frame structure, the range light always either stood on higher ground than the beacon or was itself of a greater height. Consequently, its focal plane — the height of the light above the water — was always higher than the beacon's. A mariner could gauge his position in a channel by the relation of the lights to each other. If he saw the range light directly over the beacon light, he knew he was in the center of the channel. But if the range light appeared to the right or left of the beacon, he then knew he was either to the right or to the left of center. These range lights were arranged in sets of two structures, as seen at the Chapel Hill Range in Sandy

Hook Bay. Occasionally ranges had three lights; the Horse-shoe Range East Group along the Delaware River, for example, had a common rear range for two front lights that marked the channel in both directions.

Lighthouses were also built in a variety of ways. In New Jersey, many early lighthouses, such as Bergen Point and Passaic lights, were constructed on stone cassions. In this type of construction, the courses of foundation stone were laid directly on the reefs that the lighthouses marked. While these bases offered great structural integrity, they also posed to engineers the problem of working with cement at water level and dealing with the changing tides.

Lighthouse engineers subsequently introduced the cast iron caisson, which was floated to its station preassembled, lowered underwater, and dug into the bottom of the ocean floor. Some caissons were sunk twenty feet into the seabed, others thirty-five or forty, based on the type of seabed, whether scouring currents were a factor, and whether bedrock had been struck. The cast iron caissons were then filled with concrete to provide a solid base on which to construct a tower and dwelling. West Bank Light in New York Harbor and Miah Maull Shoal Light in Delaware Bay are examples of cast iron towers built on cast iron caissons. Often, as in the case of West Bank Light, many tons of rip-rap were placed around these stations to stabilize and protect them from waves.

Other lighthouse sites had different difficulties, and needed different solutions. The screwpile foundation was ideal for soft, muddy bottoms that would not support the great weight of a stone caisson. In this type of construction, metal pilings with augers at their ends were literally screwed into the seabed to provide a piling foundation. The tower would then consist of an open framework supporting the keeper's quarters at the lower level and the lantern room at the top. The second Brandywine Shoal Lighthouse, built in 1848 and taken down in 1914, was New Jersey's only screwpile lighthouse and the first in the nation.

The Light

Lighting methods and apparatus for towers varied in fuels and efficiency of design. The earliest navigational aids date from the third century B.C., when Egyptians and Romans built open fires on hills facing the sea or developed crude systems of elevating a flame to the top of a pole. The most noted of the ancient lighthouses is The Pharos tower, which was built between 283 and 277 B.C. This structure — one of the seven wonders of the world — stood on the island of Pharos near the harbor of Alexandria. It reached a height of five hundred feet, an elevation achieved by no other structure until the late nineteenth century. In its lantern room, a wood-burning fire produced a sizable flame that, with the aid of reflectors, could be seen for miles.

This is a sixth order Fresnel range lens, originally from Chapel Hill Rear Range Lighthouse.

In eighteenth-century lighthouses, the light often consisted of a series of ordinary candles housed in lanterns that protected the wicks from wind and water. Candles were easy to maintain and clean to work with, but they did not produce a high-intensity light. Some lighthouses used a spider lamp, which consisted of four wicks protruding from a container of sperm whale oil. However, these lamps emitted smoke and fumes and were difficult to maintain. Also, due to supply and demand, whale oil became increasingly expensive, and less

This is a sixth order lens which occupied the South tower of Twin Lights from 1949 to 1952.

expensive oils were unavailable in sufficient quantities.

The first improvement in lamp technology came in 1781 with the development of the Argand lamp. (It finally arrived in the United States around 1810.) This incandescent vapor lamp used kerosene, which eliminated the smoke and fumes and allowed air to flow through the wick to make the flame brighter. Used with a parabolic reflector, the lamp produced a concentrated beam of light. But the reflector, which was crucial to the light's success, could be easily damaged.

In 1822, Augustin Fresnel developed a lens that became the highest standard in lighting. The Fresnel (pronounced "fray-nel") lens had both dioptric and catadioptric prisms above and below a central magnifying lens, creating a "bee hive" appearance. The prisms sent a concentrated beam through the lens, which had either a smooth surface (emitting a fixed beam of light) or a surface broken into bulls-eyes, each of which emitted a flash as the lens rotated. The magnifying lens both increased the size of the light and intensified its brightness.

The strength of Fresnel lenses was gauged by "order" — first, second, third, three and a half, fourth, fifth, and sixth — with the power of the lens decreasing as the numbers increased. Harbor lights contained fourth-order Fresnel lenses, while major seacoast lights such as Barnegat held first-order lenses. Some of the largest first-order lenses — which could be seen up to 20 miles away — had rotating mechanical clockwork drives and weighed over ten tons. These mammoth lenses were so perfectly balanced they could be rotated easily by hand.

In 1886, the introduction of electricity eliminated much of the maintenance in keeping a light, and ultimately led to the automation of lighthouses.

Lightship Illumination

The first lighting apparatus on lightships was the spider lamp, which was raised and lowered by a pulley system on the mast for lighting and servicing. (A crew member might also climb the mast to perform those duties.) Due to its use of liquid fuel, the lamp was suspended by a pivoting system to compensate for the rocking and swaying motion of the vessel.

As in lighthouses, kerosene lamps with parabolic reflectors eventually replaced the crude spider lamps. Later, acetylene gas replaced oil. The flow of acetylene was controlled through valves, which made the gas easier to regulate and allowed for more distinctive light characteristics, such as flashing and occulting. By the 1930s, electricity had replaced acetylene.

In addition to their lighting, these ships could also be distinguished by their colors and their markings. Early lightships had various hull colors — black, straw, green, red, even checkered — all of which contained various markings in either black or white lettering. In 1945, the Coast Guard settled on a red hull with a one-word identification name painted in white, so mariners could distinguish these ships from other vessels. In addition, colorful, cage-like daymarks in various shapes and sizes were suspended between the lightships' masts for further identification.

Automated Tower

Today, many stations are occupied by steel skeleton towers equipped with automated lights — an example of where modern technology has taken lightstations. A light of this design requires no keeper or keeper's dwelling and is a sharp contrast to the structures of old. However, while the era of keepers has come to a close, the twenty-six New Jersey lighthouses that still stand today do not mark their stations as tombstones. Rather, they stand as monuments, commemorating the reliability, faithfulness, and courage of those who once tended their lights and guided mariners to safety.

LIGHTHOUSES and LIGHTSHIPS
of NEW JERSEY

*Numbers correspond to fold-out map
on facing page*

1	STATUE OF LIBERTY		*27	LUDLAM BEACH
*2	BERGEN POINT		28	HEREFORD INLET
*3	PASSAIC		29	CAPE MAY
4	ROBBIN'S REEF		*30	FIVE FATHOM BANK LIGHTSHIP
5	ROMER SHOAL		31	EAST POINT
6	WEST BANK		*32	EGG ISLAND
7	OLD ORCHARD SHOAL		*33	COHANSEY
8	GREAT BEDS		34	FINNS POINT
9	SANDY HOOK		*35	FINNS POINT BEACON
*10	EAST BEACON		*36	DEEP WATER POINT RANGE
*11	WEST BEACON		*37	DEEP WATER BEACON
*12	SANDY HOOK LIGHTSHIP		*38	MIFFLIN BAR CUT RANGE
*13	SCOTLAND LIGHTSHIP		39	TINICUM RANGE
14	AMBROSE LIGHTSHIP		*40	BILLINGSPORT LIGHT
15	AMBROSE TOWER		*41	HORSESHOE RANGE EAST GROUP
16	TWIN LIGHTS		42	SHIP JOHN SHOAL
*17	BAYSIDE BEACON		43	ELBOW OF CROSS LEDGE
*18	WAACKAACK		44	CROSS LEDGE (caisson)
*19	POINT COMFORT BEACON		*45	UPPER MIDDLE LIGHTSHIP
20	CONOVER BEACON		46	MIAH MAULL
21	CHAPEL HILL RANGE		47	BRANDYWINE SHOAL
22	SEA GIRT		*48	BRANDYWINE LIGHTSHIP
23	BARNEGAT		*49	NORTHEAST END LIGHTSHIP
24	BARNEGAT LIGHTSHIP			
*25	TUCKER BEACH			
26	ABSECON			

* Asterisk indicates lighthouse or lightship of the past. Lightship stations are no longer occupied by vessels, but the existing lightships are at maritime museums.

Map of the Lighthouses and Lightships of New Jersey

N

Passaic River

Hudson River

3
1
2
4 BAYONNE

STATEN
ISL.

8
7
6
5

19 17
18
10
20 11
16
21 9

SANDY
HOOK

14 15

12
13

enlarged on other
side of map

I-195

22
SEA
GIRT

GARDEN STATE PARKWAY

24

23

LONG BEACH
ISLAND

25

26
ATLANTIC CITY

Lighthouses
and
Lightships
of New Jersey

⬤ *Existing Lighthouse*
◼ *Lighthouse of the Past*
◭ *Lightship Station*
----- *Range Lights*

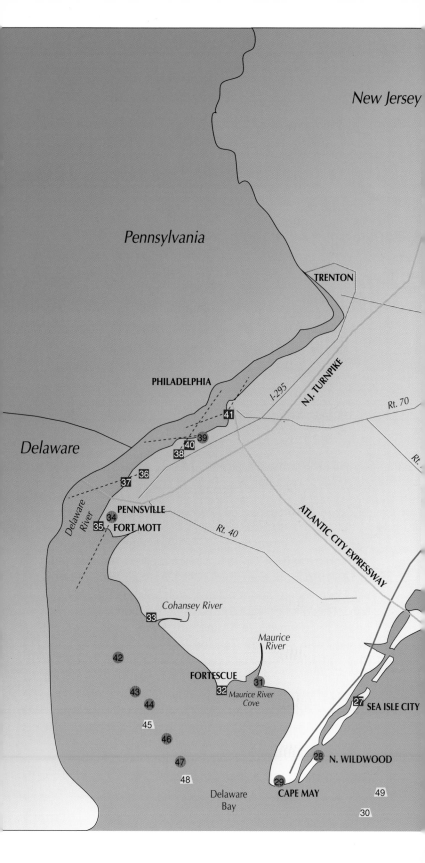

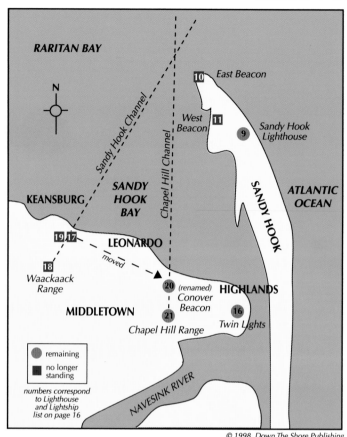

RARITAN BAY

N

Sandy Hook Channel

Chapel Hill Channel

10 East Beacon

West Beacon

11

9 Sandy Hook Lighthouse

SANDY HOOK

ATLANTIC OCEAN

KEANSBURG

SANDY HOOK BAY

19 17

LEONARDO

moved

18

Waackaack Range

20 (renamed) Conover Beacon

HIGHLANDS

MIDDLETOWN

21

Chapel Hill Range

16 Twin Lights

remaining

no longer standing

numbers correspond to Lighthouse and Lightship list on page 16

NAVESINK RIVER

Range Lights of Sandy Hook Bay

Two major channels located in Sandy Hook Bay were marked by sets of range lights which were established in 1856. To mark the Chapel Hill Channel, the Chapel Hill Light, located on a hill in Middletown, is the rear light. This aligned with the Bayside Beacon on the beach in Leonardo. In Keansburg, the Waackaack Light aligned with the Point Comfort Beacon near the shore. This range marked the Sandy Hook Channel. The wooden Point Comfort Beacon was eventually replaced by a cast iron beacon. The Sandy Hook Channel range lights were discontinued, but the 45-foot tall cast iron beacon was moved to Leonardo to replace the old Bayside Beacon. It was renamed Conover Beacon. Today, the Chapel Hill Lighthouse and the Conover Beacon still stand, but no longer function.

THE SENTINEL

by Bill Gately

One hundred years had long since passed
the building stood dark and silent
Clouds above were moving quite fast
far below the sea raged violent

Upon the bluff where children once played
around the tower's dwelling
Tall grasses in the sea breeze swayed
faint sounds of distant gulls yelling

Some pictures hung on plastered walls
a large table saw many a feast
Bedrooms are quiet, and through the halls
a draft caused by wind from the east

No keeper will climb the winding stair
of the old gray granite tower
No beam will pierce the black night air
to guide ships through darkest hours

Why the building remains is a mystery
it is not needed anymore
The lighthouse has become a part of history
a sentinel standing near the shore

Lighthouses
and
Lightships
of New Jersey

STATUE OF LIBERTY

1886

The Statue of Liberty is not initially recognizable as a New Jersey lightstation. Also known as "Liberty Enlightening The World," it is more popularly viewed as a symbol of freedom and welcome to those from other lands who wanted to make a better life. It is also viewed as a New York landmark, though it actually stands in New Jersey waters. But for fifteen years, since its establishment in 1886 on Bedloe Island in Upper New York Harbor, the Statue of Liberty served as a navigational aid. Although located in the harbor, it could be seen from twenty-four miles at sea. The light in the torch rose 305 feet above sea level and was the first beacon to be lit by electricity.

In 1901, maintenance costs and hazards within the structure ended the statue's role as a lighthouse. In 1986 a major renovation project restored the exterior for the statue's 100th anniversary.

BERGEN POINT LIGHTHOUSE

1849, 1859

In 1849, the first Bergen Point Lighthouse was established on a rocky reef off Bayonne; there it marked the entrance to Newark Bay, where the bay met the Kill Van Kull. However, that original lighthouse — a two-story, wood-frame structure with the tower rising from its center — and the pier on which it stood were poorly constructed, and within a few years Bergen Point Light rapidly deteriorated.

In 1859, a second, superior, Bergen Point Lighthouse was built on the reef. This time, instead of rising from a pier supported by rock and pilings, the new lighthouse rested on a cylindrical stone caisson. Upon this stable base, a square brick tower standing about forty feet tall held the light to mark this important shipping channel. In addition, the tower had attached to it a two-story, peaked-roof, wooden dwelling, built in Victorian style. The dwelling was L-shaped, and the light tower stood inside the L. The light had a focal plane of 53 feet, and its visibility was ten miles.

The Bergen Point Lighthouse functioned until 1948, when it was demolished during a major dredging and channel-widening project.

PASSAIC LIGHTHOUSE

1849, 1859

In 1849, the first lighthouse in Newark Bay, near the Passaic River, was established on a pier. Similar in design to the first Bergen Point Lighthouse, Passaic Light deteriorated just as rapidly in a couple of years. As a result, the U.S. Army Corps of Engineers decided to demolish Passaic Lighthouse and build a sturdy, more durable lightstation.

In 1859, the same year Bergen Point Light was rebuilt, the second Passaic Lighthouse was constructed on a cylindrical stone caisson similar to Bergen Point's. The tower was a square, wood-frame structure painted white, with a black lantern room. The attached dwelling was a two-story, peaked-roof, wood-frame house in the Victorian style. As with the Bergen Point, the tower was attached to the L-shaped dwelling, standing inside the L. The light had a visibility of ten miles.

Passaic Light became obsolete when the Passaic River changed its course and mariners no longer needed it. The lighthouse was demolished in the 1930s.

ROBBIN'S REEF LIGHTHOUSE

1839, 1883

About two miles southwest of the Statue of Liberty and just off Bayonne is Robbin's Reef. The first lighthouse to mark this navigational hazard was established in 1839. It was an octagonal stone tower, painted white, with a light that stood sixty-six feet above the water. This lighthouse was torn down and replaced in 1883 by one with a prefabricated cast iron superstructure. (The introduction of this new iron gave a boost to lighthouse builders, because it reduced construction time and costs.) The lighthouse's cylindrical caisson, however, was still built of stone. Today this is the only lighthouse in New Jersey waters that stands on a stone caisson. (The rock structure protruding from the base of the caisson formed a cove that provided welcome refuge for keepers approaching the tower in the busy harbor.)

Robbin's Reef Lighthouse is nicknamed "Katie's Light" after its best-known keeper. Jacob Walker, one of the early light keepers, and his wife, Kate, began living at this station in the 1880s. However, Jacob soon became seriously ill and was hospitalized, and his wife had to take over as keeper after his death in February 1890. Tending the light and raising their two children was now all up to Katie. She rowed the children to Staten Island in the morning to go to school, then returned to her post to maintain the light. Reportedly, Katie Walker was just under five feet tall and weighed barely a hundred pounds. However, she is credited with saving at least fifty lives in the harbor during her thirty-three years at this lighthouse.

ROMER SHOAL LIGHTHOUSE

1838, 1898

For vessels approaching the New Jersey-New York Harbor area from the ocean, Ambrose Tower is the first light to be seen, marking the beginning of Ambrose Channel. By following the channel to a point two miles due north of the northern tip of Sandy Hook, you come to the Romer Shoal Lighthouse.

Located on the left side of Ambrose Channel, where the channel turns right toward the Verrazano Bridge, this shoal was the location of an unmanned daymark in 1838. The shoal was later named after the *William J. Romer,* a vessel that sank there in 1863. As shipping increased in this waterway, it became

necessary to have more than a daymark here. So, in 1898, a red-and-white harbor lighthouse was established to house a fourth-order Fresnel lens, which had a focal plane of fifty-four feet.

Little change occurred until 1966, when the light became automated, and it continued to signal boat and shipping traffic for many years. However, the December storm of 1992 damaged the interior of the lighthouse, and the Coast Guard planned to dismantle the structure and replace it with a steel skeleton tower. However, after taking a closer look at the light, the Coast Guard decided that it could be restored.

WEST BANK LIGHTHOUSE

1901

Approximately two miles northwest of Romer Shoal Lighthouse is the region known as the West Bank. This shallow area, which extends from the opening called the Narrows down along the Staten Island shoreline, is about one and one-half miles in width. Here stands the West Bank Lighthouse, a New York light that, along with the Staten Island Lighthouse, forms a range marking the Ambrose Channel. It has been included in this text

because it marks approaches to both New Jersey and New York.

The cast iron tower has a focal plane of fifty-nine and one-half feet, and the tower's base is a pneumatic caisson. This type of foundation was built by lowering the caisson to the shoal bottom and filling it with concrete. A shaft with an airlock ran down the center of the caisson, enabling builders to descend to a pressurized chamber under the concrete-filled-structure. There they could actually dig the enormous caisson into the bay's bottom to a depth of twenty feet. After the caisson reached the desired depth, the chamber and air shaft were also filled with concrete.

Surrounding the lighthouse base are tons of rip-rap rock which serve as a wave and ice breaker.

OLD ORCHARD SHOAL LIGHTHOUSE

1893

To the south-east of Staten Is-land is a shallow area known as Old Orchard Shoal. In 1893, a white cast iron lighthouse was established on the outer edge of the shoal. Stand-ing on a cast iron caisson and sur-rounded by protective rip-rap, the tower marked the shoal's edge for vessels entering New York Harbor and heading toward Perth Amboy and the Arthur Kill. This lighthouse also formed a range with the Waackaack ("Way cake") rear light in Keansburg.

Although Old Orchard Shoal Light has guided ships for many years, its history began with tragedy. Alfred Carlow, the first keeper at Old Orchard Shoal, had previously been stationed on Sandy Hook Lightship and Scotland Lightship, "outside" stations in the open ocean. He had served well on both stations — which is to say a lot, since long hours and severe weather made lightship duty highly demanding. After serving at Old Orchard Shoal for nine years, however, he became mentally ill because of the isolation of the tower. He was hospitalized and never returned to active lighthouse duty.

Today, the lighthouse still sends its signal to mark the shoal. The focal plane of the light is fifty feet.

GREAT BEDS LIGHTHOUSE

1880

In 1880, an iron tower lighthouse was established in Great Beds, a shallow area in the center of Raritan Bay, one-half mile from the wetlands of South Amboy. The tower — called Great Beds Lighthouse — is composed of five sections, stands forty-two feet high, and has a focal plane of fifty-seven feet.

A wooden lightship designated LV 15 figures in the construction of Great Beds Light. By 1877, the forty-year-old lightship had deteriorated to a point where the Lighthouse Service determined it "not worth the cost of repair." The seventy-three-foot-long lightship was then purchased by the contractor for Great Beds Lighthouse and used as a barracks for the construction crew.

The lighthouse today is painted white, but archival photos show either a brown or a black tower on a black caisson. The white tower provides a better daymark against the background in this area.

THE BEACONS OF SANDY HOOK

1817

Sandy Hook is a seven-mile-long peninsula extending northward along the coast and forming the Sandy Hook Bay area to the immediate west. The peninsula has been connected to the mainland at Sea Bright for many years, but old maps show a cycle of changes that involved separation from the mainland

The North Beacon, or "Little Red Lighthouse", in its present location on the Hudson River in New York

and growth at the northern end. These changes affected the beacons that were placed close to the water's edge.

In addition to the Sandy Hook Main Light (Sandy Hook Lighthouse), two beacons once stood on the sea and bay coasts of the peninsula. Both beacons began operating in 1817 and ranged with buoys serving as channel lights.

The East Beacon was a wooden tower built on a stone foundation. In 1867, a frame building with an attached tower replaced the original structure, but it burned to the ground in the same year. Beach erosion nearly undermined a third attempt at the East Beacon in 1869, and the structure was moved five hundred feet south. In 1880 a thirty-five-foot cast iron lighthouse was established farther inland, away from the eroding beach, and it became known as the North Beacon.

In 1917, the North Beacon was replaced by a thirty-five foot skeleton tower, and the lighthouse was moved to Jeffrey's Hook on the Hudson River. At its new location, the lighthouse became obsolete after the construction of the George Washington Bridge, which had its own navigational lights and dwarfed the little structure: The suspension bridge towers rose six hundred feet, fifteen times the height of the lighthouse. In 1951, the Coast Guard decided to remove the "Little Red Lighthouse," as it had come to be called, but after a protest by the nation's schoolchildren, the tiny lighthouse was saved. In 1982, the New York City Park Service restored the lighthouse.

The West Beacon had to be moved when waves undermined its foundation in 1817. Jetties were built at the new site to prevent erosion, and the beacon was moved in from the bay's edge and south of its original location. Renamed the South Beacon, it ranged with Sandy Hook Main Light to mark a channel. This light was discontinued in the early 1920s and dismantled.

SANDY HOOK LIGHTHOUSE

1764

The oldest operating lighthouse in America is located on the northern end of Sandy Hook. Established in 1764 by Isaac Conro (two lotteries were held to raise money for its construc-

tion), the lighthouse is in remarkably good condition given its age and history. During the Revolutionary War, for example, the British occupied Sandy Hook Light in an attempt to control New York Harbor, and the colonists attacked the tower with cannon fire. But the lighthouse withstood the assault.

Originally just a harbor light, the tower was fitted with a third-order lens in 1856, increasing its visibility to fifteen miles. During the war with Spain in 1898 and during World War II, the light was darkened. Other than those two periods, the lighthouse has served continuously for 232 years.

SCOTLAND LIGHTSHIP STATION and BUOY 2A

In 1866, the steamer *Scotland* rammed another vessel a few miles off Sandy Hook. The rammed vessel sank immediately and the *Scotland* followed soon afterward, posing a great navigational hazard. In 1868, a lightship was established near the site to warn mariners, but it was moved after the wrecks were towed to deeper water in 1870. The station, however, had become a well-known point of reference for navigators, and in 1874, a lightship was stationed there once again. From 1868 until 1962, several lightships occupied this position that became known as the Scotland Lightship or the Wreck of the Scotland Lightship station.

In 1962, a large, automatic navigation buoy was anchored at this spot to replace the much more expensive lightship. Designated 2A, the buoy had a light that rose nearly forty feet above the water, a racon (radio beacon), and a fog signal. The buoy's cylindrical central column allowed personnel access to the light and other instruments above. The deck of the buoy was round, and the bowl-shaped bottom had compartments for ballast and fuel storage. All together, the low-profile platform, cylindrical tower, and hinged number signs offered little wind resistance.

This forty-foot buoy was eventually replaced by one about half that size. (Two similar large buoys along the coast, one at the Five Fathom Bank station and one at the Delaware Lightship station, have since been replaced with smaller ones as well.) The problem with the big buoys is that they cannot be lifted to a ship's deck for maintenance. The sheer weight of the buoy (one hundred tons), plus all of the sensitive equipment on board, makes a lift impossible. Also, an overhaul for a large buoy costs about $100,000 every five years, while a smaller buoy requires about $1,000 in maintenance for the same time span. The present buoy at the Scotland Lightship station contains a Japanese-designed wave generator and solar cells that continually recharge the twelve-volt battery. The battery operates the light, fog signal, and racon. The base is nine feet wide and stands twenty-one feet above the water. (The large navigational buoy from the Delaware station contains three diesel generators for operating the equipment. The buoy holds enough fuel to run for a year, and when fully fueled and ballasted weighs 100 tons.) Although the smaller buoys do not have the same range of weather instruments, they serve well to mark their positions.

VESSELS OCCUPYING THE WRECK OF THE SCOTLAND STATION

LV 20   1868-1870
         1870-1874 (discontinued)
LV 23   1874-1876
LV 20   1876-1880
LV 7   1881-1902 (in 1891 station renamed Scotland)
LV 11   1902-1925
LV 69   1925-1936
LV 87/WAL 512 1936-1942
Buoy - WWII   1942-1945
LV 78/WAL 505 1945-1947
LV 87/WAL 512 1947-1962

LV = Light Vessel; WAL = W used to distinguish Coast Guard from Navy designations, and then WAL replaced LV. Source: Flint, Index - 026, 027.

AMBROSE LIGHTSHIP

1908 - 1967

Established in 1823, the Sandy Hook Lightship station was the first oceanic lightship station in the United States. In 1908, the station was moved to mark the entrance of Ambrose Channel (which leads into New York Harbor) and renamed Ambrose. In 1967, the lightship was replaced by Ambrose Tower, ending the station's 144 years of service — a record for a lightship.

The first vessel at the Ambrose station was the steel- hulled LV 87, built in Camden in 1907 by the New York Shipbuilding Company for ninety-nine thousand dollars. With a length of more than 135 feet and a beam of 29 feet, it displaced 683 tons. This was the first lightship to have a radio beacon; installed in 1921, the new technology enabled ships to home in on a signal rather than to rely on visual aids. The 87 served at Ambrose from 1908 to 1932, when she was donated to the South Street Seaport Museum in New York City. The next vessel to mark Ambrose was LV 111, stationed there from 1932 to 1952.

A Coast Guard-built lightship, WLV 613, was the last vessel stationed at Ambrose, serving from 1952 to 1967. This lightship had a tripod mast instead of the conventional single stem structure. Although replaced by the automated tower, a signal is still sent to mark this important navigational location.

Lightships were exposed to the fury of the sea, but sufficient moorings, such as 5,000- or 7,500-pound mushroom anchors, and stabilizing broad-based hulls and bilge keels prepared these vessels for the worst conditions. Ironically, advancing technology placed lightships in harm's way even further: Shipping traffic homed in on a lightship's radio beacon until they were quite close to the station — sometimes too close. For example, in June 1960, the 613 was in Staten Island for routine repairs, and a relief vessel, LV 78, was assigned the post temporarily. On the night of June 24, a thick fog rolled in, and the cargo carrier *Green Bay* fixed on the lightship's signal for guidance. But the carrier miscalculated the distance to the lightship and ran into it, sinking the relief vessel. (LV 78 weighed 668 tons, which seems a substantial size, but freighters could weigh in at 10,000 tons.) Fortunately, all nine crewmen aboard the relief vessel were picked up by a motor launch from the *Green Bay*. Today, the old lightship remains upright and intact in 110 feet of water just east of Ambrose Tower.

VESSELS OCCUPYING THE SANDY HOOK STATION

VV	1823-1829
	1829-1839 (discontinued)
WW	1839-1854
LV 16	1854-1891
LV 48	1891-1894
LV 51	1894-1908 (in 1908 station moved and renamed Ambrose)

VESSELS OCCUPYING THE AMBROSE STATION

LV 87/WAL 512	1908-1932 (photo)
LV 111/WAL 533	1932-1952
WLV 613	1952-1967

LV = Light Vessel; WAL = W used to distinguish Coast Guard from Navy designations; WLV = Designation for Coast Guard-built lightship. Source: Flint, index—026

AMBROSE TOWER

1967

In 1967, the $2.5 million Ambrose Tower, built in Texas-oil-rig style, replaced Ambrose Lightship. The tower's platform or deck rises ninety feet above the water and holds the keeper's quarters and storage tanks. The light tower rises another forty-six feet, creating a focal plane of 136 feet. The signal, a six-million-candle-power white strobe light, flashes every 7.5 seconds. The light is so powerful that it can be seen from shore even on bright, sunny days.

At the waterline of Ambrose Tower is a bumper railing for boat landings. A walkway leads to the structures's northwest leg, which has a spiral staircase winding up to the platform. During the era of lighthouse keepers, a lifeboat hung from two davits on the west side of the upper platform.

The legs of this structure are imbedded about 170 feet into the sea floor. This open design allows waves to pass under the station and minimizes damage, vibration, and noise. It is estimated that this tower can withstand 125-mile-per-hour winds and sixty-five-foot waves.

Ambrose Tower's keepers were transported to and from the structure by helicopter until 1988, when the tower became automated. This was not just another automation of a lightstation, though: It marked the end of lighthouse keepers in the waters of New Jersey.

TWIN LIGHTS OF NAVESINK

(NAVESINK LIGHTHOUSE)

1828, 1862

In 1828, on one of the highest points along the coast, the first Twin Lights of Navesink were established. The octagonal towers stood forty-six feet high and more than three hundred feet apart; the north tower had a fixed light, while the south tower light rotated. In 1841, French-designed Fresnel lenses — the first used in America — were installed at Navesink. However, by 1851 the towers had begun to crumble and needed replacement.

This is a sixth order fixed Fresnel lens, which currently occupies the North tower at Twin Lights.

In 1862, with their lights standing nearly 250 feet above Sandy Hook Bay, the new brownstone towers were completed. Considering the era, the builders accomplished quite a feat to bring the massive amount of stone to such a height for construction. In 1898, a generator was in-

stalled, making Twin Lights the first major seacoast light to use electricity. At the turn of the century, Navesink was considered the best and most powerful light in America, with a brightness of 25 million candlepower and a visibility of more than twenty miles. Ironically, it was also at this time that the north tower light was turned off, after the federal Lighthouse Board began to question the effectiveness of "twin lights." (There were seven twin light stations, all in the Northeast.)

In 1939, the U.S. Coast Guard absorbed the Lighthouse Service. Under Coast Guard jurisdiction, the Twin Lights of Navesink was decommissioned in 1949 as newer navigational equipment made the lighthouse obsolete. Today Twin Lights is a museum of lighthouse and life-saving-station artifacts maintained by the State of New Jersey Division of Parks and Forestry.

The octagonal north tower, which is connected to the museum and open to the public, contains a sixth-order Fresnel lens. From the top of the tower a viewer can see Sandy Hook Light and several of the other New York Harbor lights, including Ambrose Tower.

The south tower contains no lighting apparatus, but once held a first-order, rotating bivalve lens. The square tower is connected to the brownstone keeper's dwelling, which is 228 feet long. Although still referred to as Twin Lights, the lighthouse is actually one building. When it was in operation, the lightstation had up to five keepers — a head keeper and four assistants assigned to the watches —and the dwelling consisted of eighteen rooms.

CHAPEL HILL LIGHTHOUSE

1856

At an elevation of 224 feet above sea level, the Chapel Hill Rear Range Lighthouse stands about one and a half miles south of Conover Beacon, which is located on the beach in Leonardo. These two lighthouses, both wood-frame structures, formed the Chapel Hill Range. Conover Beacon was later replaced by Bayside Beacon, which was moved from Keansburg and renamed Conover (see next page).

Chapel Hill Lighthouse is the last wooden rear range light

of its kind in New Jersey. It is almost a duplicate of the Point Comfort Beacon, which stood in Keansburg . Chapel Hill Lighthouse has a chimney at each end of the building, and a square tower surmounts the center of the roof. This lighthouse was decommissioned in the 1940s and replaced by an automated tower.

CONOVER BEACON

1856, 1930s

A wooden tower once stood on the beach at Point Comfort in Keansburg. Approximately one-half mile southwest of this Point Comfort Beacon was Waackaack ("Way cake") Rear Range Light, an open-frame tower. Together the two lights formed a range to mark Sandy Hook Channel. The Point Comfort Beacon was eventually replaced with a metal tower and renamed Bayside Beacon.

In Leonardo, established in 1856 right on the beach, was a wooden front light called Conover Beacon. About one and a half miles to the south stood Chapel Hill Rear Range Lighthouse. The Chapel Hill light ranged with Conover Beacon to mark Chapel Hill Channel.

In the 1930s, the Waackaack rear light was decommissioned and dismantled. The Bayside Beacon was moved to the Conover site to replace the old wooden structure, and it was renamed Conover Beacon. In the 1940s, an automated steel tower replaced Chapel Hill Light, and the tower continued to range with Conover Beacon.

CHAPEL HILL LIGHT TOWER

1940s

This white steel tower stands about 200 feet north of the old Chapel Hill lighthouse, which the tower replaced in the 1940s to continue marking Chapel Hill Channel. The automated tower stands in a heavily wooded area and was discontinued in the 1950s. This light and its range partner, Conover Beacon, were both fixed lights. Conover Beacon, the steel tower, and Chapel Hill Lighthouse all remain standing today.

SEA GIRT LIGHTHOUSE

1896

In 1896, a square, red-brick tower with a keeper's dwelling was established close to the beach at Sea Girt. This point was chosen both to mark the local inlet and to light up an area between Navesink and Barnegat lights. Although Navesink and Barnegat were major seacoast lights, the distance between them

left mariners out of view of both at certain distances from shore. With its fourth-order lens, Sea Girt Lighthouse maintained the mariner's continuity of signals.

In 1921, Ambrose Lightship and Fire Island Lighthouse in New York were the first lightstations in the world to have a radio beacon installed. These three positions marked approaches from the north, the south and the trans-Atlantic. During World War II, Sea Girt's light was darkened, but the Coast Guard used the lighthouse as a headquarters for patrolling the beach against invasion and as a lookout for U-boats. The light was decommissioned in 1945.

In 1956, the Borough of Sea Girt purchased the lighthouse for eleven thousand dollars. In 1981, the Sea Girt Lighthouse Citizens Committee was established to restore and preserve the structure. The committee leases the building from the town and raises funds for its preservation. The interior of the lighthouse has been beautifully restored and furnished in keeping with its historical period.

BARNEGAT LIGHTHOUSE

1835, 1859

Barnegat Lighthouse is perhaps the most familiar feature of the New Jersey shore. The handsome red-and-white tower stands at Barnegat Inlet as a symbol of the state's maritime heritage. In 1988, the lighthouse was restored, and it is now open to the public on a seasonal basis.

In the age of sail, New York and Philadelphia were major ports for trans-Atlantic shipping. The fortieth parallel crosses the New Jersey coastline about sixty miles south of New York Harbor, about sixty miles north of the Delaware Bay entrance, and about a mile north of Barnegat Inlet. This location was a crucial navigational point for trans-Atlantic travel. In addition, the inlet needed to be marked for local shipping. A shoal area extended from shore and posed a coastal hazard, a fact recognized by Dutch explorers who named Barnegat Inlet "Barendegat," or "place of the breakers." The need for a good light at this location became evident as shipwrecks occurred frequently in the vicinity, yet Barnegat was without a lighthouse until 1835.

In 1820, Congress appointed Stephen Pleasonton as a full-time supervisor of lighthouses, but it was 1834 before he decided to have a lighthouse built at Barnegat. The first lighthouse stood forty feet high, and its light consisted of eleven lamps with fourteen-inch reflectors.

Initially there were many complaints by ship captains concerning Barnegat Lighthouse. They noted that the height of the tower and the lighting apparatus were insufficient. In conditions of poor visibility, Barnegat's beacon was often mistaken for another vessel's light, and mariners came dangerously close to shore looking for the signal that was intended to guide them to safety. At Twin Lights of Navesink, a second-order lens had been installed in 1841, and the light was regarded as the best in New Jersey. In 1854, a fourth-order Fresnel lens was installed at Barnegat. Though an improvement, the light still did not serve well as a major seacoast beacon. Also, beach erosion had begun to endanger the brick lighthouse.

In 1855, Lieutenant George Meade, a government engineer, estimated that as many as six thousand ships passed through the Barnegat area in a year. He recommended that nothing less than a first-order light should be there. Meade had already designed Absecon Lighthouse, which held a first-

---

BARNEGAT LIGHTHOUSE LENS

This Fresnel lens is from Barnegat Lighthouse and is now located in the Barnegat Light Museum. It was built in 1847 outside of Paris in the St. Gabian Works. The five-ton lens, which consists of more than a thousand prisms held together by a massive brass frame, was rotated by a clockwork mechanism and turned on bronze rollers. The twenty-four bulls-eyes

located around the central band of the lens produced a flash every ten seconds; each flash lasted 2.5 seconds, and the lens took four minutes to make a single revolution. The lens stands approximately ten feet tall and has an inner diameter of seventy-two inches. The light it produced was so intense that it could be seen up to thirty miles away. It is believed that the light could have been seen at greater distances, but it was limited by the Earth's curvature.

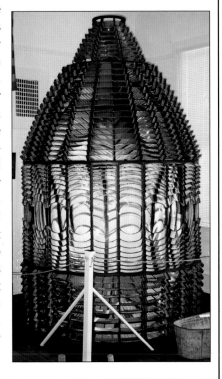

---

order lens at a height of 167 feet. The same style and quality of lighthouse was to be erected at Barnegat.

Between 1856 and 1859, a new lighthouse was built about 900 feet south of the original light. The tower held a first-order rotating Fresnel lens, with a focal plane of 165 feet. The nearby keeper's dwelling was a two-and-a-half-story frame building with three separate living quarters for the keeper, his two assistants, and their families.

Over a period of years, the newly constructed seacoast light became endangered by erosion. The original tower, which had been abandoned after being replaced, ultimately collapsed into the sea, and a second battle near the new tower was almost lost after a series of jetties failed to control the erosion. In the 1930s, the federal government joined forces with the State of New Jersey, building a bulkhead around the tower and dredging the inlet to slow the current.

Barnegat Lighthouse became automated in 1927, the same year that Barnegat Lightship began serving at its station eight miles off the coast. In the early 1940s, the lightship was designated to mark Barnegat Inlet and offshore waters, and the lighthouse was decommissioned. The tower had functioned from January 1, 1859 to January 1, 1944. Today its first-order lens and other artifacts are on display at the Barnegat Lighthouse Museum.

BARNEGAT LIGHTSHIP

1927-1969

Barnegat Lightship, established in 1927 about eight miles east of Barnegat Inlet, was a "leading mark" to follow from Northeast End Lightship (off Cape May) to Ambrose Lightship (off Sandy Hook). Since the signal from Barnegat Lighthouse was not always visible in dense fog, the lightship helped vessels stay clear of shoals.

The vessel that served as Barnegat Lightship from 1927 to 1967 was LV 79. (During its last two years, this station was occupied by LV 110.) LV 79 was built in Camden in 1904 by the New York Shipbuilding Company for eighty-nine thousand dollars. A steel-hulled vessel, it measured 129 feet long, with a twenty-eight-foot, six-inch beam; a twelve-foot, six-inch draft; and a displacement of 668 tons. Before serving off Barnegat Inlet, LV 79 served on Five Fathom Bank off Cape May and as a relief vessel.

The ship's illuminating apparatus changed with the advances in lighting technology. Originally each mast held a cluster of three oil lens lanterns, as they were called. In 1921, the oil lens lanterns were replaced by 375-millimeter acetylene lens lanterns, and by 1928 these were converted to electricity. In 1931 the lightship -— which had been originally powered by a steam engine — was refitted with a diesel engine.

The lightship station was considered to be a more effective light than Barnegat Lighthouse. On January 1, 1944, Barnegat Lighthouse was decommissioned. The lightship station continued its duties until 1969, when the vessel was replaced by a lighted horn buoy.

VESSELS OCCUPYING THE BARNEGAT STATION

LV 79/WAL 506	1927-1942 (photo)
Buoy during WWII	1942-1945
LV 79/WAL 506	1945-1967
LV 110/WAL 532	1967-1969

LV = Light vessel; WAL = W used to distinguish Coast Guard from Navy designations. Source: Flint, index-028.

TUCKER BEACH LIGHTHOUSE

1849, 1879

At the southern end of Long Beach Island, a series of storms in the winter of 1800 cut an inlet to Barnegat Bay, creating an eight-mile-long island. Also known as Tucker's Island or Tucker Beach, the island had its first lighthouse established in 1848. The structure, a one-story brick building, held what was reported to be a dim light, one not as bright as those carried by passing vessels. In 1859, the Tucker Beach Light was discontinued; by then the first-order light of Absecon had been lit, making the smaller lighthouse obsolete. However, in 1867 a fourth-order Fresnel lens was installed at Tucker Beach, and the tower became operational again. For many years it served as a continuation light between Barnegat and Absecon.

The sea, meanwhile, had eroded Tucker Beach until the island was only a mile long. But life along the island continued. In 1879, the wooden, two-story keeper's dwelling was expanded and fitted with a square, block tower projecting from the center of the roof. A fourth-order Fresnel lens was installed in it, and the old tower was converted to an oil shed. The new lighthouse was painted white and had a porch facing the sea.

By 1927, the sea had undermined the building, and the lighthouse had to be abandoned. In October the lighthouse tumbled into the sea, and over the next twenty-five years the other island buildings, including a Coast Guard station, a schoolhouse, and islanders' homes all met the same fate. Ultimately the island disappeared completely, but it has occasionally resurfaced at the whim of ocean tides and currents.

ABSECON LIGHTHOUSE

1857

Prior to 1857, no major seacoast light marked the dangerous shoals of Absecon and Brigantine near Atlantic City. That changed with Absecon Lighthouse. Lieutenant George Meade, who later oversaw the construction of Barnegat and Cape May lighthouses, was the engineer in charge of Absecon's construction. The foundation of the lighthouse was placed on the sand dunes close to the water, giving the 159-foot tower a focal plane of 165 feet. The illuminating apparatus was of the highest order: a fixed first-order Fresnel lens, from Paris.

Originally the tower was painted white with a red band in the center. In 1898, the color scheme was changed to an orange tower with a black central band — perhaps because of some initial confusion between Absecon and its "sister" lighthouse at Barnegat, which was so close in size and color. Eventually Absecon's original color scheme — white tower with red band — was reinstated, and it remains today.

Decommissioned in 1933, the lighthouse now stands in the middle of a park. The lighthouse is undergoing restoration by the Inlet Public-Private Association (IPPA), a group composed of business leaders and community members dedicated to promoting the redevelopment of the inlet section of Atlantic City.

LUDLAM BEACH LIGHTHOUSE

1885

The original location of Ludlam Beach Lighthouse was seventeen miles south of Absecon Lighthouse and eleven miles north of the Hereford Inlet light. Ludlam marked a shoal area off Townsend Inlet and also served as a continuation light between Absecon and Hereford stations, similar to the role of Tucker Beach Lighthouse between Barnegat and Absecon.

The lighthouse was built on a barrier beach only a few feet from the ocean, and it had a focal plane of forty feet. The one-story, wooden building had a roof ridge that ran parallel to the shoreline, and the tower was built on the beach side of the roof. The light was produced by a fourth-order, rotating Fresnel lens, creating a flashing signal.

In 1889, a storm nearly destroyed the lighthouse when pounding waves seriously undermined the building. A bulkhead was constructed to help protect the vulnerable station, and the lighthouse subsequently stood for many years. Through that time it had only one keeper, making it unique among lighthouses. Joshua H. Reeves was an assistant keeper at Barnegat Lighthouse until 1885, when he was transferred to be head keeper at Ludlam. Reeves remained at Ludlum until his retirement in 1924, the year the lighthouse was decommissioned. The building was sold and moved to Sea Isle City; the lighthouse tower was removed, and the building is now a private residence. An automated steel tower was built at the lighthouse's former site and it remains there today.

HEREFORD INLET LIGHTHOUSE

1874

Located in North Wildwood, the Victorian-era Hereford Inlet Lighthouse stands complete with gingerbread porch railings and louvered shutters. It is prominently positioned in the dune area overlooking the inlet, which lies nearly equidistant from Great Egg Harbor to the north and the mouth of Delaware Bay to the south. This location has made the inlet an inviting shelter for intracoastal traffic.

In 1964, the Coast Guard darkened the Hereford light and built this automated tower with a modern optic. In 1982 the Hereford Inlet Lighthouse was restored and its original fourth order lens put on display in the dwelling part of the lighthouse. The modern optic was removed from the automated tower and placed in the lantern room of the lighthouse in 1986 and, by popular demand, the steel tower was taken down.

The station, built under the supervision of the U.S. Army Corps of Engineers, has five fireplaces and, during its decades of operation, provided considerable comfort for the keeper and his family. The tower itself rises forty-nine and one-half feet from the center of the roof and has a focal plane of fifty-seven feet. Initially it contained a fourth-order, fixed Fresnel lens. Then in 1924, the lighthouse received a new rotating lens that emitted a repeating series of flashed signals, known as a "group flash." This series consisted of a white light with a red sector, which was produced by installing a red panel visible to mariners. The lens operated until 1964, when the Coast Guard decommissioned the lighthouse and built an open-frame, automated tower nearby.

In 1982, the lighthouse was turned over to the town of North Wildwood, and the original Fresnel lens was displayed in the keeper's quarters. A few years later, the light in the automated tower was removed and placed in the lantern room of the lighthouse. Today the lighthouse continues to serve as a museum and is maintained by the Hereford Inlet Lighthouse Commission and community volunteers.

HEREFORD INLET LIGHTHOUSE LENS

The first illuminating apparatus in Hereford Inlet Lighthouse was a fourth-order, fixed Fresnel lens that produced a white light. In 1924 a new rotating lens was installed that produced a repeated series of flashed signals, known as a "group flash." The new lens issued a white light with a red sector (produced by installing a red panel visible to the mariner from a certain area). This lens operated until 1964 and is currently on display, complete with its clockwork mechanism, in the restored lighthouse.

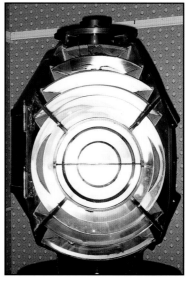

CAPE MAY LIGHTHOUSE

1823, 1847, 1859

The first documented lighthouse on Cape May Point was established in 1823. (There are references to a "flash light" during colonial times at this site, but no descriptions of a lighthouse exist.) The 1823 tower, a sixty-eight-foot conical, brick structure, had a focal plane of eighty-eight feet. Lamps and reflectors produced the light which revolved to create a flash.

By 1847, erosion had endangered the lighthouse, and a new tower was built four hundred yards northeast of the original. The second tower stood seventy-eight feet tall and had the same lighting apparatus as the first lighthouse. But reports indicate that this second structure was poorly built and leaked. In

addition, the light it produced was considered inferior. After a little more than ten years, the government decided to build a third light. Lieutenant George Meade of the U.S. Army Corps of Engineers had just completed the Absecon Lighthouse, and he was placed in charge of the Cape May Light construction. Since the tower would mark the important entrance to Delaware Bay, Meade determined that a new lighthouse of no less than 150 feet needed to be built, and that it would contain a first-order Fresnel lens: Cape May's third lighthouse was to rank with the other major seacoast lighthouses along New Jersey's coast. When completed in 1859, the new lighthouse stood 159 feet tall and its first-order lens revolved.

In 1933, the lighthouse became automated. In the 1940s the first-order lens was removed from the tower; eventually it was put on display at the Cape May County Historical Museum in Cape May Court House. Today the lighthouse contains a reflector lens and a one thousand-watt bulb and continues operation under the Coast Guard.

CAPE MAY LIGHTHOUSE LENS

Built in 1823, the first Cape May Lighthouse had a revolving illuminating apparatus that consisted of fifteen lamps with reflectors. In 1847, when a second tower was completed, the old lamps were installed. Eventually, a first-order Fresnel lens was made for the tower. The lens had a distinctive thirty-second flash produced by rotating the bullseye flash panels. The lens is now located in the Cape May Court house Museum.

FIVE FATHOM BANK AND NORTHEAST END LIGHTSHIPS

1839

Approximately fifteen miles southeast of Cape May Lighthouse was the lightship station known as Five Fathom Bank. Established in 1839, this station marked the entrance to Delaware Bay for more than 130 years.

The first lightship, a sail-rigged vessel, was not seaworthy enough for this "outside" post. The next vessel, LV 37, served from 1869 to 1876 and ultimately became the first lightship in the United States to sink at its mooring. Ironically, this happened at Five Fathom Bank during an August storm in 1893, when LV 37 was serving as a relief vessel. Only two of the six-man crew aboard the

This is the lighting mechanism on the main (rear) mast of the Five Fathom Bank Lightship (WLV 189), developed by the Coast Guard and installed on the 189 in 1966. Referred to as a "flash cube," the apparatus is four-sided, with six high intensity locomotive headlights on each side. As the mechanism turns, it produces a flash which can be seen up to fifteen miles.

lightship survived.

The most recent lightship to serve at Five Fathom Bank, WLV 189, was built in 1946. The 189 served there only one year, from 1971 until 1972, when the station was decommissioned. The lightship then served at the Boston station before being decommissioned itself and sent to Gardner's Basin in Atlantic City as a display vessel. As the 189 was being towed to New Jersey, a tanker struck her and ripped a gaping hole in her port side. The vessel was never restored and sat at the dockside for seventeen years. The rusting lightship was eventually donated to New Jersey's Artificial Reef Program, and on February 28, 1994, she was sent to the bottom.

Approximately twelve miles east of Hereford Inlet and eight miles northeast of Five Fathom Bank was the Northeast End Lightship station, so named because of its location in regard to Five Fathom Bank. The station was occupied by two vessels between 1882 and 1932 before being discontinued.

VESSELS OCCUPYING THE FIVE FATHOM BANK STATION

LV 18	1839-1869
LV 37	1869-1876
LV 39	1876-1877
LV 40	1877-1904
LV 79/WAL 506	1904-1924
LV 108/WAL 530	1924-1942
WWII buoy	1942-1945
LV 108/WAL 530	1945-1970
LV 110/WAL 532	1970-1971
WLV 189	1971-1972 (photo)

VESSELS OCCUPYING THE NORTHEAST END STATION

LV 44	1882-1926
LV 79	1926-relief vessel between LV 44 and LV 111
LV 111/WAL 533	1927-1932

LV = Light Vessel; WAL = W used to distinguish Coast Guard from Navy designations; WLv = Designation for Coast Guard-built lightship. Source: Flint, index - 029, 030

EAST POINT LIGHTHOUSE

1849

Formerly known as the Maurice River Lighthouse, East Point Lighthouse was established in 1849 on the shore of the Delaware Bay near the Maurice River. The light served faithfully until it was decommissioned in 1941, and for many years after it remained one of the region's most recognized landmarks. Then, in 1971, a fire burned the roof and lantern room and, in 1972, a storm did additional damage to the structure. The Maurice River Historical Society eventually rebuilt and restored the lighthouse to its original appearance, and the tower was fitted with a new light in 1980. This light is maintained by the Coast Guard and has a focal plane of fifty-three feet.

East Point Lighthouse is the most remote land-based light in New Jersey. The road leading to it passes miles of undeveloped land that must look much the same as it did back in 1849. The lighthouse's distinctive red roof and red lantern

room stand out clearly as a daymark; the building itself is constructed of red brick and is painted white. The view from the lighthouse grounds facing south is of Delaware Bay, and none of the offshore lighthouses can be seen from this point — revealing how huge the bay really is.

EGG ISLAND LIGHTHOUSE

1838, 1856

In 1838, a lighthouse was established on the point of marshland near the mouth of the Maurice River. This light marked the Egg Island Flats for approaching mariners and could be reached only by boat.

The original light was a two-story, wood-frame dwelling that stood on a brick pier foundation and had a black lantern room. But the building was poorly constructed, and it began to deteriorate immediately. It was replaced in 1856 by a new structure forty-five feet high, with a focal plane of fifty feet. This lighthouse served until 1939, when its lighting apparatus was removed and placed on a skeleton tower about one hundred feet away. The lighthouse was ultimately destroyed by fire in 1950.

COHANSEY LIGHTHOUSE

1838, 1883

The first lighthouse built at the mouth of the Cohansey River on upper Delaware Bay had a Cape Cod style and a lantern room similar to the one at East Point Lighthouse. In the same year the lighthouse was constructed, an inspection showed it was poorly built and already displaying signs of decay. In 1878 a storm destroyed the crumbling lighthouse.

By then the Cohansey station was already seeing the erosion that would eventually alter the shoreline.

Appropriations were made for a new lighthouse at a safer, inland location. In 1883 the lighthouse was completed: a white, wood-frame building, thirty-five feet tall, with a focal plane of forty-six feet. The lighthouse operated until 1931, when it was replaced with an automated steel tower. The 1883 building burned within a few years.

FINNS POINT RANGE

1876

The front light for Finns Point Range was a two-story, wood-frame dwelling with a square tower. This thirty-foot-tall building once stood on the marshy ground along the Delaware River in lower Penn's Neck Township; together with the rear light, it marked a nearby channel. In 1938, it was replaced by a steel skeleton tower.

The rear range tower still stands today, rising 115 feet. Built in 1876 for $1,200, it is an iron, open-frame lighthouse painted black, with a central column containing the staircase. In 1950, the channel in the river was altered, and Finns Point Range became obsolete. Restored in 1983, the Finns Point rear light is now part of the Supawna Meadows National Wildlife Refuge in Pennsville and is open to the public.

DEEPWATER POINT RANGE

1876

The Deepwater Point Range marked the channel at the upper end of Bulkhead Shoal. The front range lighthouse, established in 1876, was a two-story, wood-frame dwelling with the lantern room within a gable. Unlike most lighthouses, the lantern room was located below the ridge of the roof. A horizontal latticework above the black lantern room, together with a vertical black stripe below it, served as a daymark.

The rear range tower, similar to Finns Point Rear Range Light, stood 100 feet tall. In the late 1930s, the Deepwater lights became automated. But when the Delaware Memorial Bridge opened in 1951, it blocked mariners' view of the range lights and both lights were decommissioned the next year. Today, automated beacons continue to mark this waterway.

FORT MIFFLIN BAR CUT RANGE

1880

The Fort Mifflin Bar Cut Range marks a cut through a bar in the Delaware River. The front range light is known as the Billingsport Light. The original beacon, a white, square lantern room on an open-frame tower, served the Fort Mifflin Bar Cut Range in an upriver direction and the Tinicum Range downriver (see below). In 1908, an automated steel tower replaced this light.

The Fort Mifflin Bar Cut Rear Range Light was a white, four-sided, pyramidal tower. The lantern room was black and had a black, circular, slatted daymark above it. Around 1950, this light, too, was replaced by an automated tower. The range still functions today and is maintained by the Coast Guard.

TINICUM REAR RANGE LIGHTHOUSE

1880

Established in 1880 to range with the Billingsport Light, the Tinicum Rear Range Lighthouse rises eighty feet and has a focal plane of 112 feet. A neo-classical entry pavilion, built entirely of cast iron, stands at the base of the tower.

Located in the center of the Billingsport recreational area, the lighthouse has a fixed red signal and still ranges with the automated tower that replaced the Billingsport front light in 1908. The lighthouse is maintained by the Coast Guard and is closed to the public.

HORSESHOE RANGE EAST GROUP

1881

A set of range lights —— an upper front light, a lower front light, and a rear light —— was established in 1881 near Horseshoe Bend on the Delaware River. The upper (north) front light was a white structure that stood about six feet high. The lower (south) front light was identical to the upper except for its color, red. And the rear light was a white, four-sided, tapering wooden tower next to which stood a two-story, wood-frame keeper's dwelling. This rear light had a focal plane of fifty-two feet.

Called the Horseshoe Range East Group because they were built on the east side of the river, the three lights stood opposite the Horseshoe Range West Group in Pennsylvania, which also consisted of three structures. Together, these two groups guided ships through Horseshoe Bend. The East Group was rebuilt in 1938 as automated skeleton towers with only one front light, at the upper location.

SHIP JOHN SHOAL LIGHTHOUSE

1877

In 1797, the ship *John* was returning from Germany to Philadelphia when it wrecked on a shoal located off the mouth of the Cohansey River. Fortunately, all the passengers and crew made it safely to shore, but the vessel sank and was broken up by ice floes. The shoal was afterward known as Ship John Shoal — the name given to the lighthouse that began operating there eighty years later.

The water at this site measures a mere eight feet deep, but it wasn't until the 1870s that a lighthouse marked this danger. Originally the builders considered a screwpile structure because of the shoaling bottom, but they eventually chose a cast iron caisson filled with concrete for the foundation. Construction began in 1874, and in 1877 the permanent light was lit. Built in Second Empire Victorian style, the new lighthouse had a focal plane of fifty feet.

Over the following years, hundreds of tons of rip-rap were placed around the caisson to protect it from scouring currents

and ice floes (which continually washed away the stones). In 1894, heavier stones ranging in weight from two to six tons each were placed around the lighthouse, with openings for approaches by boat. These stones are still in place today.

Now automated, Ship John Shoal Light is still in operation. In 1989 a construction firm began major repairs on this magnificent lighthouse to save it from the harsh elements, and it has since been restored.

ELBOW OF CROSS LEDGE LIGHTHOUSE

1907

This lighthouse stood in the Delaware Bay about a mile northwest of the original Cross Ledge Lighthouse (see next page), where it marked a turn in the channel. A red-brick, octagonal tower, it stood on a cast iron caisson and had a brown lantern room.

After being damaged by a hurricane in 1951, the lighthouse was automated; an underwater cable supplied the power. In 1953 the lighthouse again suffered severe damage when a freighter struck it in dense fog. The following year, an automated steel skeleton tower was assembled on the caisson. The light still shines today, with a focal point of sixty-one feet, and is maintained by the Coast Guard in Cape May.

CROSS LEDGE LIGHTHOUSE

1855, 1875

The first screwpile lighthouse in American waters was constructed in 1848 at Brandywine Shoal and it immediately proved a success. Based on this success, a similar lighthouse was planned at Cross Ledge. However, after work began in 1855, ice floe activity destroyed the foundation work.

In 1875, a two-story, wood-frame dwelling with a mansard roof and a black lantern room was constructed at Cross Ledge on a granite pier, replacing the Upper Middle Lightship station (see below). However, after the construction of Elbow of Cross Ledge Lighthouse in 1907, Cross Ledge Lighthouse itself was discontinued.

All that remains of Cross Ledge Light now is the granite pier which is listed on charts as "Abandoned Lighthouse." Ironically, the site of this former aid to navigation is today considered a hazard since the pier is not marked or lighted.

UPPER MIDDLE LIGHTSHIP

1823

The Upper Middle Lightship station began operating in 1823 and marked the area known as Cross Ledge. The first vessel to occupy this station was one of the earliest lightships in America. Built in New York in 1823, it was designated Lightship X. Much smaller than later lightships (such as Ambrose's LV 87 which weighed in at 683 tons), the X was a wooden-hulled vessel seventy-two feet in length, with a twenty-foot beam and a weight of 120 tons.

The heavy ice floe activity each winter posed a particular problem to all stations in Delaware Bay, lighthouses and lightships alike. In the frigid winter of 1874, moving ice pushed the Upper Middle Lightship off its station; the following year, the lightship was replaced by Cross Ledge Lighthouse. The lightship was moved to Fourteen Foot Bank, where it served until 1887, when a lighthouse again replaced it.

VESSELS OCCUPYING THE
UPPER MIDDLE (CROSS LEDGE) STATION

X   1823-1845
LV 19   1845-1875
Source: Flint, index-034

MIAH MAULL
LIGHTHOUSE

1913

The last offshore lightstation established in Delaware Bay was constructed at Miah Maull Shoal, southeast of Egg Island Point. The shoal is named after Nehe-miah Maull, who drowned there in an eighteenth-century shipwreck.

Miah Maull Lighthouse is a cylindrical, cast iron tower painted red; it stands in nineteen feet of water and has a focal plane of fifty-nine feet. Like the Ship John, Elbow of Cross Ledge, and Brandywine Shoal lights, Miah Maull stands on a cast iron caisson filled with concrete, the design best suited for this waterway. The light was automated in the early 1970s and continues to function today.

BRANDYWINE SHOAL LIGHTHOUSE

1828, 1848, 1914

In 1828, a piling-built lighthouse was established on Brandywine Shoal, but it was destroyed by the sea within a year. A lightship designated Lightboat Brandywine was then anchored at the shoal until a second lighthouse could be completed in 1848. This second light was the first constructed in the United States with a screwpile design. Introduced by an Irish marine engineer, Alexander Mitchell, this design featured auger-tipped metal pilings that were literally screwed into the seabed to provide a foundation. (Mitchell developed the design from his experiments with methods for anchoring ships.) Brandywine Shoal also had an iron fence built around its base, to protect the pilings from destructive ice floes.

The lighthouse lasted remarkably well, but after about sixty years saltwater had corroded the ironwork of the foundation pilings. The lighthouse was replaced in 1914 by a reinforced concrete lighthouse built on a cast iron caisson. The lighthouse still stands today.

VESSELS OCCUPYING THE BRANDYWINE SHOAL STATION

N   1823-1850
Also referred to as LIGHTBOAT BRANDYWINE and as BRANDYWINE No. 1. *Source: Flint, index - 032*

REFERENCE
SECTION

LOCATIONS OF REMAINING LIGHTHOUSES AND LIGHTSHIPS

SANDY HOOK LIGHTHOUSE
Take Garden State Parkway to exit 117, then Route 36 over Highlands Bridge; turn right as soon as you cross bridge. Gateway National Recreation Area, Sandy Hook.

AMBROSE LIGHTSHIP LV 87
South Street Seaport Museum
207 Front St.
New York, N.Y. 10038
(212) 669-9400

TWIN LIGHTS OF NAVESINK
Take Garden State Parkway to exit 117, then Route 36; turn right immediately before the Highlands Bridge. Very steep driveway.

CONOVER BEACON (BAYSIDE)
Take Garden State Parkway to exit 117, then Route 36 to Leonardo. Follow signs to Leonardo State Marina.

CHAPEL HILL LIGHTHOUSE
Private residence.

SEA GIRT LIGHTHOUSE
In the town of Sea Girt, take Beacon Boulevard off Ocean Avenue.
(732) 974-0514

BARNEGAT LIGHTHOUSE
Take Garden State Parkway to exit 63 (Long Beach Island), then Route 72 east over the Manahawkin Bay Bridge on to Long Beach Island; turn left when Rt. 72 ends, then continue on Long Beach Boulevard to the north end of the island, to Barnegat Lighthouse State Park.

Barnegat Lighthouse State Park
P.O. Box 167
Barnegat Light , N.J. 08006
(609) 494-2016

BARNEGAT LIGHTSHIP

Pyne Poynt Place (Yacht Basin)
75th Street on Delaware River
Camden, N.J. 08102
(609) 966-1352

ABSECON LIGHTHOUSE

Take Garden State Parkway to exit 38, then Atlantic City Expressway to Atlantic City. Take Pacific Avenue to the corner of Pacific and Rhode Island avenues.

HEREFORD INLET LIGHTHOUSE

First and Central avenues
North Wildwood, N.J. 08260
(609) 522-4520 or 522-2030

CAPE MAY LIGHTHOUSE

Mid Atlantic Center for the Arts
Cape May Point State Park
Cape May Point, N.J. 08204
(609) 884-5404

EAST POINT LIGHTHOUSE

Located at mouth of Maurice River along the Delaware Bay.
Maurice River Historical Society
210 N. High Street
Millville, N.J. 08332
(609) 327-3714
E-mail: windchim@cyberenet.net

FINNS POINT REAR RANGE LIGHTHOUSE

Supawna National Wildlife Refuge
Pennsville, N.J.
(609) 935-1487

TINICUM REAR RANGE LIGHTHOUSE

Located near the recreational area, next to a ball field, in Billingsport, which is west of Paulsboro. Use Route 130 along Delaware River.
Coast Guard phone for further information: (215) 271-4847

OFFSHORE LIGHTHOUSES
NEW YORK/NEW JERSEY AREA

STATUE OF LIBERTY
Located near the mouth of the Hudson River in New York Harbor.

ROBBIN'S REEF LIGHTHOUSE
Near Bayonne in Upper N.Y. Harbor.

ROMER SHOAL LIGHTHOUSE
Two miles north of Sandy Hook.

WEST BANK LIGHTHOUSE
Four miles north of Sandy Hook.

OLD ORCHARD SHOAL LIGHTHOUSE
Two miles off Great Kills Harbor, Staten Island, Lower N.Y. Harbor.

GREAT BEDS LIGHTHOUSE
A half-mile off South Amboy.

AMBROSE TOWER
Ten miles east of the northern tip of Sandy Hook.

OFFSHORE LIGHTHOUSES
OF DELAWARE BAY

BRANDYWINE SHOAL LIGHTHOUSE
Located about seven miles west of Cape May Point.

MIAH MAULL SHOAL LIGHTHOUSE
Located about seven miles south of Fortescue Marina.

CROSS LEDGE CAISSON
Located about five miles southwest of Fortescue Marina.

ELBOW OF CROSS LEDGE
Located about four miles southwest of Fortescue Marina.

SHIP JOHN SHOAL LIGHTHOUSE
Located about ten miles northwest of Fortescue Marina.

Note: All five Delaware Bay offshore lighthouses mark the main shipping channel in the bay.

BIBLIOGRAPHY

Annual Report of the Lighthouse Board for the fiscal year ending June 30, 1890. Washington: Government Printing Office, 1890. pp. 21, 58 map, 63-70, 84 map, 85-87, 91-92, 229-237

Annual Report of the Lighthouse Board for the fiscal year ending June 30, 1898. Washington: Government Printing Office, 1898. pp. 73-75, 79, 82, 95-98, maps.

Bachand, Robert G. *Northeast Lights: Lighthouses and Lightships Rhode Island to Cape May, New Jersey.* Norwalk, Connecticut: Sea Sports Publications, 1989.

Duffy, Francis J. and William H. Miller. *The New York Harbor Book.* Falmouth, Maine: TBW Books, 1986.

Farner, Thomas P. *New Jersey in History: Fighting to Be Heard.* Harvey Cedars, New Jersey: Down The Shore Publishing, 1996.

Findlay, Alexander G. *The Lighthouses of the World, Coast Fog Signals and Tides.* London: Richard Holmes Laurie, 1899-1900.

Flint, Willard. "Illumination and Signaling Systems,"*The Keeper's Log,* vol. 6, no. 2 (Winter 1990), pp. 13-15.

Lightships and Lightship Stations of the United States Government. Printed by the Coast Guard Historian's Office, U.S. Coast Guard Headquarters, Washington, D.C.

Gowdy, Jim. *Guiding Lights of the Delaware River and Bay.* Mizpah, N.J.: self-published, 1990.

Holland, Francis Ross, Jr. *America's Lighthouses: An Illustrated History.* New York: Dover Publications, 1988.

Great American Lighthouses. Washington, D.C.: The Preservation Press, 1989.

Lloyd, John Bailey. *Six Miles at Sea: A Pictorial History of Long Beach Island.* Harvey Cedars, New Jersey: Down The Shore Publishing, 1990.

———. *Eighteen Miles of History on Long Beach Island.* Harvey Cedars, New Jersey: Down The Shore Publishing, 1994.

Methot, June. *Up and Down The Beach.* Navesink, New Jersey: Whip Publishers, 1988.

Naish, John. *Seamarks.* London: Stanford Maritime, 1985.

Putnam, George R. "Beacons of the Sea." *National Geographic Magazine,* Washington, D.C.: vol. 24, no. 1 (January 1913), pp. 1-53

Roberts, Bruce and Ray Jones. *Northern Lighthouses New Brunswick to the Jersey Shore.* Connecticut: The Globe Pequot Press, 1990.

Savadove, Larry and Margaret Thomas Buchholz. *Great Storms of the Jersey Shore.* Harvey Cedars, New Jersey: Down The Shore Publishing, 1993.

Snow, Edward Rowe. *The Lighthouses of New England.* New York: Dodd, Mead and Company, 1984.

Witney, Dudley. *The Lighthouse.* New York: Arch Cape Press, 1989.

Worthylake, George. "Only Yesterday." *Keeper's Log,* vol. 8, no. 1 (Fall 1991), pp. 22-23.

RELATED PUBLICATIONS OF INTEREST

The Keeper's Log
This is a quarterly publication of the United States Lighthouse Society. Wayne Wheeler is the founder and president of this organization, which has thousands of members. This magazine is a must for anyone interested in lighthouses and lightships.

> United States Lighthouse Society
> 244 Kearney Street
> Fifth Floor
> San Francisco, California 94108

The Beam
This is the quarterly newsletter published by the New Jersey Lighthouse Society. This publication covers lighthouses, with an emphasis on those of New Jersey. Also, lighthouse tours by land and by chartered boat give members the opportunity to observe these historic structures up close.

> New Jersey Lighthouse Society Inc.
> P.O. Box 4228
> Brick, New Jersey 08723

Shore Village Museum Newsletter
Located in Rockland, Maine, the Shore Village Museum is the best lighthouse museum in the country. It is owned and maintained by Ken Black. A newsletter containing book lists, updates on current lighthouse and lightship preservation projects, and lighthouse-related topics is available.

> Shore Village Museum
> 104 Limerock Street
> Rockland, Maine 04841
> (207) 594-0311

Lighthouse Digest
Published by Tim Harrison, this magazine contains approximately thirty pages of lighthouse articles, history, current restoration projects, replica collectibles, gifts, and book lists. Published each month.

> Lighthouse Digest
> P.O. Box 1690
> Wells, Maine 04090
> (207) 646-0515

ACKNOWLEDGMENTS

I would like to express my sincere thanks to the individuals and organizations who helped me in obtaining information and enabled me to photograph some of the offshore stations.

First, I would like to thank the Coast Guardsmen at the Sandy Hook station for the trip to Ambrose Tower and for their courtesy in answering my many questions. The New Jersey Lighthouse Society provided the means for photographing the Delaware Bay lighthouses. Thanks to Captain Bob Layton for the excellent tour of the Delaware Bay lights aboard his boat, the *Mariner.*

Thanks to Jim Gowdy, a lighthouse historian, for his information on the past lighthouses of the Delaware Bay region. His book, listed in the bibliography is, in my opinion, the definitive work on that region. Thanks to Tom Laverty and his assistants at Twin Lights for arranging permission and providing assistance in photographing the various lenses. Thanks to Wayne Wheeler, president of the United States Lighthouse Society, for providing information on New Jersey's past lightstations.

I owe a great deal to my two editors, Marion Figley and Rich Youmans, for their thorough work in structuring this book and for their ideas and suggestions. Also, I must thank my publisher, Ray Fisk, for accepting my book and making all of this possible.

My biggest thanks is to my wife, Linda. Her help with the photography alone was priceless. Her encouragement helped much.

Thanks to each and every person mentioned here, and I pray that this book concerning New Jersey's lighthouses and lightships can be of some value to anyone interested in the subject.

Bill Gately, a director of the New Jersey Lighthouse Society and member of the United States Lighthouse Society, has spent over a decade researching the state's lightstations. He began his work not only to satisfy his own fascination with these landmarks, but to fill a gap in the state's recorded history. This book now fills that gap, and readers can for the first time see just how varied the state's lightstations have been. As he writes in his introduction, the twenty-six lighthouses still remaining in New Jersey do not stand as tombstones to a faded past, but as "monuments commemorating the reliability, faithfulness, and courage of those who once tended their lights and guided mariners to safety."

Down The Shore Publishing offers many other book and calendar titles (including the annual New Jersey Lighthouse Calendar). For a free catalog, or to be added to the mailing list, just send us a request:

Down The Shore Publishing
P.O. Box 3100, Harvey Cedars
New Jersey 08008